Is it Wise to Specialize?

What Every Parent Needs to Know About Early Sports Specialization and its Effect Upon Your Child's Athletic Performance

By John O'Sullivan
Author of the Bestselling Book *Changing the Game*

About the Author

John O'Sullivan is the author of the bestselling book *Changing the Game: The Parent's Guide to Raising Happy, High-Performing Athletes and Giving Youth Sports Back to Our Kids*. He is the Founder of the Changing the Game Project, and his writing has been featured in the Huffington Post, Soccer America, and The Soccer Wire. John is also a nationally known speaker and coaching educator, working with schools and youth sports organizations, as well as speaking at TEDx Bend in 2014. He teaches parents and coaches how to create a player-centered youth sports environment, be better leaders for our children, and create model youth sports organizations that put our players first.

John spent nearly three decades as a soccer player and coach at the youth, college and professional level, most recently as the Central Oregon Regional Training Center Director for the Portland Timbers of Major League Soccer. He holds a USSF A License, USYS National Youth License, and NSCAA Advanced National Diploma. He is a 1994 graduate of Fordham University and received his Masters degree from the University of Vermont.

Table of Contents

Introduction

In 1974 a boy was born in Johannesburg, South Africa, and soon immigrated to Canada. Growing up he had aspirations of being a professional soccer player. Then, at age thirteen, he got his first basketball, which he described as "finding a new friend." Already years behind many of his peers in terms of practice and competition, he took to the game wholeheartedly and in eighth grade he told his mother he was going to one day play in the NBA. He was right.

Despite starting basketball five to eight years after most American and Canadian boys, Steve Nash went on to become one of the most skillful basketball players of all time, a two-time NBA MVP, and a perennial all-star. In his words, as quoted by David Epstein in The Sports Gene, "If you are good at other sports, you can translate it easily to any sport at that age. I realized when I was about thirteen or fourteen that I had a chance to be a really good [basketball] player."

As a young athlete, Steve Nash and many future elite athletes like him had a period of sports "sampling" years. These athletes tried many activities until they found one that suited them physically, socially and psychologically. In their book Raising Your Game, authors Ethan Skolnick and Dr. Andrea Corn interviewed over 100 professional athletes. They discovered many stories of multi-sport backgrounds similar to that of Nash. For example, tennis great Roger Federer's parents often pushed him…to take tennis less seriously![1]

Despite these stories, **conventional wisdom in youth sports today seems to be pushing the vast majority of children down a path of early sport specialization**. There is a movement to do more, more, more at younger and younger ages. There is a hyper-focus on the few things an athlete gains by early specialization, instead of what he or she loses, as well as a litany of physical, psychological and social consequences. Athletes are being forced to commit to a single sport before they have the time to sample many, and the maturity to know if it is the right sport for them.

Is this the right path?

Before I answer that, I want to state unequivocally that I believe sport has the ability to have a massive, positive impact upon the lives of children and the overall health of our nation. Unfortunately, today in the United States, sport is failing. As stated by The Aspen Institute's Project Play Initiative:

> Largely gone is the era of the sandlot or pickup play. Today, adult-led competition dominates and tryout-based, multi-season travel teams form as early as age 6. Support has shifted away from in-town recreation leagues as well as school P.E., recess and intramurals, often the only sport options for the economically or physically disadvantaged, the child of a single parent, the late bloomer, and the kid who needs exercise as much or more than any other – the clinically obese. **One-third of all children today are overweight or obese, six**

times the rate of the 1970s.

Only three in ten kids between the ages of 6 and 17 regularly play sports, according to the Sports & Fitness Industry Association. In schools serving low-income youth, only 1 in 4 students play sports, according to 2012 research conducted for the Robert Wood Johnson Foundation. In wealthier areas, school and club-based sports have grown – many kids enjoy the experience – but so, too, have concerns about concussions, burnout and dubious motivational techniques used by untrained volunteers. A survey by the American College of Sports Medicine found that while 91 percent of Americans believe sports are important to the development of children, 94 percent say more needs to be done to protect their health and safety. Parents, coaches and leaders want solutions, but do not know what those are or where to turn.[2]

One of the answers parents are looking for is when to specialize in a sport. Each and every day in my role as the Founder of the Changing the Game Project, whether it is in an email, an interview, after a speech I give, or simply from friends and family who have children in sports, I am asked some form of the following questions:

"When should my son pick a sport if he wants to play in college?"

"Is it too early to specialize?"

"We are getting pressure to pick one sport, but my daughter loves them all. What do we do?"

I am here today to tell you that I cannot answer those questions for you.

What I can do is give you the latest research into long term athletic development, psychology, as well as the sociology and medical research surrounding youth sports. Only you know your child. What this booklet will give you are the tools to make an informed decision and answer these types of questions for yourself.

Unfortunately, there is a lot of misinformation out there. It is my sincere hope that what you read here will help you weed through that misinformation. I hope it will give you the tools to take a stand against organizations, coaches and other parents that may be preaching a sport development plan that does not fit your needs or those of your child.

By the end of this booklet, you will have an understanding of the difference between a single versus a multi-sport development plan. You will have the latest science on the medical issues faced by single sport athletes as opposed to multi-sport participants. You will be aware of the psychological and social development issues that many single sport athletes face. You will have a realistic picture of the sporting backgrounds of many of today's top athletes, and the chances of your child advancing to play a sport beyond high school. Perhaps you will have even considered the true purpose of sport in your child's life, and asked yourself "is his current athletic experience serving that purpose?"

Ultimately, I hope you will have the tools to answer the crucial question:

"Is it time, and is it wise, for my child to specialize?"

Let's get started.

What Exactly is "Early Sport Specialization?"

According to researchers Joseph Baker, Stephen Cobley and Jessica Fraser-Thomas in their paper "What Do We Know About Early Sport Specialization? Not Much!" there are four required elements for an athlete to be considered an early specialist:

1. Early starting age in a sport
2. Early involvement in a single sport instead of diversification
3. Early intense, focused training
4. Early involvement in competition[3]

In their review of the existing studies on early specialization versus diversification, Baker, Cobley and Fraser-Thomas found that the case for early specialization seems compelling at first glance, due to the strong relationship between time spent practicing and achievement. It seems logical that everything else being equal, the more practice an athlete has, and the younger he or she starts, the more of an advantage he or she gets over others that start later or have not trained as much. This so called "10,000 Hour Rule" has become accepted as a fact of elite athletic development, despite the fact that the man who is given credit for 'discovering" the rule, Anders Ericsson, has come out against applying it to sports, or even calling it a rule.

Many researchers have also found compelling evidence highlighting a relationship between early sport specialization and negative consequences in physical, psychological and social development. There is little doubt that excessive training at an early age can certainly improve sports performance early on, but at what costs? And do those costs negatively affect sports development in such a way that a path of sampling and diversification is a far better one to pursue if one hopes to be an elite athlete?

Let's Look at the Science

To answer the question of "when should my child specialize?" we must first delve into the science and psychology of youth sports and child development. Until I began researching and writing my book Changing the Game, and doing extensive research for my live events and blogging, I was not aware of the insightful information that was out there, information that radically altered my thinking not only as a coach, but as a father.

As such, I believe that before you make an informed decision as important as whether to pursue single or multiple sports, you must have an understanding of the following items:

1. The science and best practices of Long Term Athletic Development (LTAD)
2. The latest research into injury rates among single and multi-sport athletes
3. The alarming burnout and dropout rate in youth sports today
4. The role of deliberate practice and deliberate play in athlete development

LTAD: The Blueprint for Athlete Development

Long Term Athletic Development refers to the framework of athlete education and development that can be used to teach our parents, coaches, and administrators about optimal ways to educate and develop high-performing athletes. LTAD focuses on developmental rather than chronological age and links athlete education with their physical and psychological growth, as opposed to calendar years. Developed in part by internationally recognized coaching educator Istvan Balyi, the LTAD model aggregates widely accepted principles of athletic development that have been the basis of physical education for years. Over one hundred major national and international sporting federations have adopted the principles of LTAD as the basis for new player and coaching education programs.[4]

The main goal of LTAD, and Canadian Sport For Life, the program charged with instituting it throughout Canada, is to develop physical literacy in young athletes (twelve and under). Physical literacy is defined as acquiring the fundamental movement skills and sports skills that need to be *learned* as a child, so that children will feel good about participation in physical activities. Note that there is emphasis on learned, as not all children have these skills innately, nor do they come as easily for some as they do for others. They must be taught.

Physical literacy involves learning the ABCs of agility, balance, coordination, and speed so that children possess the ability to move confidently and appropriately on the field or in the arena of their chosen sport or activity. The goal is to increase ability in all types of athletic activity, for the science shows that when children become more competent, they participate more vigorously, play for longer durations, and perform better.

As a parent of a young child, it is imperative that you put them in an environment that teaches the movements and skills of physical literacy. This does not mean only organized sports programs. This can be backyard play, running and jumping at the playground, swimming or sledding with the family, or riding your bikes. In the first three stages of LTAD (ages 0-12), parents are at the forefront in promoting physical literacy. Some kids figure these movements and skills out on their own. Others do not and must be taught and encouraged to learn.

CS4L has **broken up long-term athletic development into seven stages** based upon the newest science, research, and on-the-ground experience in athletics, coaching, and education. Their methodology demonstrates that by introducing and training the correct skills at the right times of development, both kids and adults will become more active, stay active, and perform better than those who do not follow such a program. The seven stages are:

1. Active Start (ages 0-6)

2. FUNdamentals (girls 6-8, boys 6-9)

3. Learn to Train (girls 8-11, boys 9-12)

4. Train to Train (girls 11-15, boys 12-16)

5. Train to Compete (girls 15-21, boys 16-23)

6. Train to Win (girls 18+, boys 19+)

7. Active for Life (any age)

The first three stages are designed to teach children physical literacy. These stages teach movement and sport fundamentals before children reach puberty so that they have the basic skills needed to remain active for life. They also provide a foundation for elite-level competition at the older ages if that is the path the child chooses.

Stages 4-6 are for the elite training of athletes. They are for children who choose to focus on a specific sport or sports and are designed to maximize the physical, mental, and emotional development of each athlete. Stage 7 is focused on taking these properly developed athletes and making them lifelong participants in recreational and competitive sports, as well as promoting an active lifestyle.

Without getting into too much depth here, if your child is not involved in an early specialization sport such as figure skating or gymnastics, **the first three stages are about sampling a wide variety of sports, and developing overall athleticism.** Kids should be changing activities season to season to avoid burnout and boredom. These activities can be structured but should still focus on FUN; competitive games and matches should be kept to a minimum. Kids begin to read the game going on around them and thus can make decisions, and movements, based upon what is happening during the match. Let them see the game, and try not to see it for them!

These are times when children are **sensitive to developing agility, balance, coordination, as well as hand and foot speed through fun activities and games**, and not necessarily training regimens and drills. Every sport can develop these skills, and even a soccer coach can be working on catching while jumping, running, even doing forward rolls. If your child has a preferred sport, there is nothing wrong with him participating two to three times a week, but make sure he is doing other sports or activities three times a week as well. This well-rounded approach helps to master all aspects of physical literacy and keeps the child excited and engaged.

That said, medical practitioners and child psychologists recommend that a child should participate in organized athletic training and competition in **an amount of hours equal to or less than the child's age**. A 10 year old should not have more than 10 hours of structured sports in any week (whether it is one sport or multiple sports). Don't make your child a multi-sport specialist!

The **Learn to Train Stage** (girls ages 8-11 and boys ages 9-12) is an age where children begin to convert their foundational movements into basic sports skills, a stage which CS4L calls the "Golden Age of Learning." If you think about it, this makes perfect sense as this stage comes to a close when the child hits puberty, the growth spurt occurs, and there is a temporary loss of coordination and motor control. This is the best time to learn sport-specific skills as the child is still in control of his body and can see daily and weekly improvement from his hard work. This is the sensitive period of accelerated skill development and must not be overlooked or shortchanged by overemphasizing competition (as often happens).

Unless your child is doing an early specialization sport, such as gymnastics or skating, they should still participate in a wide variety of sports during this stage. That said, they can begin to focus on developing sport-specific skills during those training hours. The emphasis should continue to be on more training and less competition, with at least a 2:1 or 3:1 ratio of practice to games. This is a great time to develop strength, flexibility, and some stamina, but through relays, fun activities, and training without supplemental weights instead of physically demanding regimens.

One very interesting thing to note about the Learn to Train stage is that it can be either a great advantage to a late-developing athlete or a great disadvantage. With excellent coaching, in a proper development environment, a young athlete who hits puberty later than her classmates has a longer period in which to develop fundamental and sport specific skills. She remains in the "Golden Age" longer than her peers, and if she takes advantage of this extra time, her technical skill base can surpass the early developers.

Unfortunately, oftentimes late developers are overlooked for select-level sports teams simply because they have not grown, they are not as strong, and they are not as fast. The overemphasis on competition at these young ages funnels out these late developers as coaches pick the biggest and strongest players for success in competition. This is a worrying trend, for studies show that over the long term the late developers who are kept within the high-level training regimen become better long-term performers because of a better skill base (to read more on this, read my blog post "Our Biggest Mistake: Talent Selection Instead of Talent Identification."

If your child is in this stage, and she is a late developer, make sure she is in the right coaching and developmental environment. She should continue to focus on her skills and not things like strength and speed, which will come naturally a bit later. Many times as a soccer club director I saw parents trying to get their late-developing son to lift weights and get stronger so they could play against the big guys, when the focus should have been on doubling down on the skill development. Five years down the road, the kids with the extra skill are now the same size, the same speed, and are usually the better players.[5]

The big takeaway from the studies of LTAD, and its successful implementation in many countries across a variety of sports, is that for the vast majority of athletes, especially those in popular team sports such as soccer, hockey, basketball, baseball and football, a **multi-sport background seems to produce the type of all around athleticism that future elite competitors need.** It also allows a child, such as a young Steve Nash, to **find a sport that best suits their physical, psychological, and social skills**.

(If you would like to learn more about these seven stages, I recommend Istvan Bayli's Long Term Athlete Development, or visit CS4L's website www.canadiansportforlife.ca)

Medical Studies on Early Sport Specialization

A massive body of evidence is emerging regarding the physical issues that can be caused by early sport specialization, including a higher rate of overuse injuries, reduced motor skill development, and a range of risks associated with musculoskeletal, nutritional, cardiac and sexual maturation issues. Every year, millions of children seek medical attention for sports injuries, and nearly half of those are caused by overuse.

In a widely cited 2013 study of 1200 youth athletes, Dr Neeru Jayanthi of Loyola University found that early specialization in a single sport is one of the strongest predictors of injury. Athletes in the study **who specialized were 70% to 93% more likely to be injured** than children who played multiple sports![6]

There is also an alarming rise in sport specific injuries in very young athletes, such as elbow and shoulder issues in baseball pitchers that were rarely seen before the age of early specialization. World renowned orthopedist Dr. James Andrews has noted a tenfold increase in the need for ulnar collateral ligament reconstruction – aka Tommy John surgery – over the last decade. He found that **pitchers who compete in leagues more than eight months a year were five times more likely to need the surgery by the age of 20! He also found that pitchers who regularly threw with tired arms were 36 times more likely to have surgery!** The main risk factors, according to Andrews, were playing year round baseball, fatigue, and pitchers who constantly threw at maximum velocity. In other words, get rid of the radar guns, and play other sports![7]

Concussions have become another major issue in youth sports. Every day we are learning more about the long term effects of childhood head trauma.[8] Again, children who are most at risk are those who repeatedly put themselves in situations to get concussions and absorb multiple blows to the head.

One of the most common characteristics amongst children who get injured early and often is single sport specialization. Why? Because single sport athletes usually overemphasize competition. They also suffer often from a lack of rest, little or no periodization of activity, repeated use of the same athletic movements, and a lack of the many athletic benefits of multi-sport participation.

To conclude this section as succinctly as possible, let me say this; **I have yet to see a prominent pediatric orthopedic, or for that matter any medical doctor, come out and advocate early sport specialization as a healthy or recommended way to raise a child.** (For more on this, I recommend Until it Hurts by Mark Hyman, a fantastic piece of research on youth sports injuries.)

Burnout and Dropout in Youth Sports

One of the most cited statistics in youth sports writing is the alarming **70% dropout rate from youth sports by the age of 13**. Three out of four children quit sports because sports are no longer enjoyable, because they are injured, and because sport no longer serves their needs. This is a major problem.

According to the Sports Fitness Industry of America, since 2007, baseball participation is down 21.7 percent; tackle football is down 13.8 percent, basketball 9.4 percent, and soccer 2.5 percent. While some smaller sports have seen increases, such as lacrosse (up 15 percent) and rugby (up 14.2 percent), millions of kids are quitting sports. In just one year, from 2011 to 2012, participation in team sports in all forms fell from 54 percent to 50 percent among children ages 6 to 17.[9]

Why is this happening?

A number of studies have tied the high dropout rate in youth athletics with early sport specialization. In sports such as hockey and swimming, researchers found that athletes who dropped out on average began specialized training earlier, did more dry land/off-ice training at younger ages than athletes who continued participation. In fact, a 1992 study of Russian national team swimmers found that those who specialized the earliest took longer to reach international status, and retired at a younger age. Even more alarming is that almost half of these swimmers were no longer involved in their sport in the ten-year follow up study! Not only did they dropout; they quit forever![10]

Burnout, the social, psychological and sometimes physical withdrawal from a formerly enjoyed activity, also seems to occur for similar reasons, namely early specialization and focus on competition. Studies on tennis players have found that these athletes felt more parental pressure, less enjoyment, and less ownership of their sports experience.[11]

Research by Dr. Travis Dorsch of Utah State University found that children were keenly aware of the time and financial commitments that parents made for sport. The greater the parental spending, the more pressure children felt, and the less enjoyment and motivation they derived from sport. This is especially true when parents expect a performance-related return on investment from their kids. Says Dorsch, ""When you take your kids to Disneyland, you hope it enriches their day—not that they'll win a competition to take Mickey Mouse home with them."[12]

Not to be overlooked are the **significant social implications** of early sport specialization. Sociologist Jay Coakley of the University of Colorado calls this one-dimensional self-concept that many athletes attain a developmental dead end, where children feel trapped in a role and identity completely associated with their sporting success. When they burnout and quit, or simply become less successful athletes, their whole social structure may crumble, and their self worth may diminish. The pressure and stress can make them quit far before they ever achieve their athletic potential.[13]

According to Dr. Joseph Baker, one of the world's leading sports scientists, children need three things in order to continue with athletics for the long term. These factors are so significant, that I would go as far as saying that without them, **there is little chance your young athlete will ever perform at his or her very best**. They are:

1. **Intrinsic Motivation**: Baker calls intrinsic motivation the "*currency of athletic performance*." If your child does not have it, not only is it very hard to instill, but your athlete will never have the drive, grit and mental fortitude to train and play hard enough. I see many parents who are the ones leading the charge when it comes to going to training, doing extra work on the side, and finding opportunities for the athlete to challenge himself and get out of his comfort zone. This does not bode well for the future of that athlete.

2. **Enjoyment**: For some reason, there are a number of misguided coaches and parents who think that competitive sports and enjoyment are mutually exclusive. They are not. In fact, if an athlete does not love her sport, if she does not enjoy the experience, she will never hang around long enough to be good. This does not mean that every single moment has to pleasurable, as I know many top athletes who might not consider conditioning training to be enjoyable. But the experience, taken as a whole, must be fun, it must keep them coming back, and it must be something they look forward to doing.

3. **Autonomy:** Your athlete must have ownership over his or her sports experience. The goals pursued must belong to them. As coaches and parents, we can suggest some goals and encourage athletes to aim higher, but ultimately we must release them to their game, and their goals. They have to drive the bus, and we must be the navigator who helps them find the way. We can encourage, we can push them

and hold them accountable for their ambitions and dreams, but ultimately, if it is you and not your kids in the driver's seat, the trip will be a short one.

No matter how much talent your athlete has, no matter what level of coaching he or she receives, or how many championships that team has won, **without intrinsic motivation, enjoyment and autonomy, your athletes will never play long enough, train hard enough, and be gritty enough to become an athlete who performs up to his or her potential.** Instead, they will likely burnout, and then drop out.

When a child is channeled into a single sport at an early age, very quickly their ownership of the experience can dissipate. As one all-star team becomes two, as one travel weekend a month becomes a weekly occurrence, and as three days a week of a sport becomes six or seven, **the child quickly loses control of his childhood!** Very soon, the enjoyment that a sport used to bring, and finally the intrinsic motivation to head out to play and practice, is gone.

In order to prevent both the psychological and physical ailments that many single sport specialists face, leading youth sports researchers Jean Cote and Jessica Fraser-Thomas go so far as to **suggest that at no time should a young athlete participate year round in a single sport.** While they recommend that athletes in sports whose competitors peak after age 20 need to accumulate around 10,000 hours of general sports participation, no more than half of that needs to be deliberate practice of their chosen sport. As a general rule they recommend the following age breakdown for athletes trying to achieve elite status in a specific sport:

- Prior to age twelve: 80% of time should be spent in deliberate play and in sports **OTHER THAN** the chosen sport!
- Age 13-15: **50/50 split** between a chosen sport and other athletic pursuits
- Age 16+: Even when specialization becomes very important, **20% of training time should still be in the non-specialized sport and deliberate play.**[14]

Deliberate Practice or Deliberate Play?

What is the role of play in the training and advancement of aspiring young players to the next level? Should they be practicing or playing sports? If they do both, is one more important than the other? These are all great questions.

The role of deliberate practice in skill acquisition is a hot topic, especially with books such as Malcolm Gladwell's Outliers and Dan Coyle's The Talent Code giving credence to the importance of focused training in attaining excellence. Simply defined, **deliberate practice is the focused improvement through repetitive activity, continual feedback and correction, and the delay of immediate gratification in pursuit of long term goals.** There is no question that expert performers accumulate many hours of deliberate practice, and there is a strong correlation between hours of deliberate practice and performance level in elite performers.

What gets lost in the focus on practice is the massive importance of deliberate play. Researcher Jean Cote defines **deliberate play as** "activities such as backyard soccer or street basketball that are regulated by age-adapted rules and are set up and monitored by the children or adults engaged in the activity. These **activities are intrinsically motivating, provide immediate gratification and are specifically designed to maximize enjoyment**." Intrinsic motivation, enjoyment, and run by kids? Play meets all three of Baker's criteria required to long term athletic participation!

The world of early sport specialization has taken the focus off of the role of play and turned the focus of the competitive youth sports world toward training and practice. I believe this is the wrong approach. Why?

First, at the **very core of great athletes is a burning passion and love of the game**. That love and enjoyment provides them with the intrinsic motivation to pursue sport excellence. While coaching can foster this love, and provide an athlete with the feedback needed to develop skill, the flame must be fed primarily by the athlete and not the coach. It must belong to him. **Play instills this type of love, while practice usually does not**.

Second, an early focus on deliberate practice and pursuit of long term success, instead of playing for the love of the game, **can cause motivation to become extrinsic, rather than intrinsic**. Athletes motivated extrinsically by championships, fame and social identity tied to athletic success have been shown to burnout at a much higher rate than athletes who participate for enjoyment. They are also **more likely to protect that identity through cheating and other maladaptive behaviors** designed to continue successful outcomes.

Third, free play and multi-sport play **promotes the development of better all-around athleticism**. As children play less and practice more (often in a single sport) using sport specific muscles and movements, experts in many sports have noticed a decline in the agility, balance and coordination skills of young athletes as compared to decades ago.

Finally, and perhaps most importantly, **play stimulates brain development**. It hastens the growth of the brain centers that regulate emotion and control both attention and behavior. Play inspires thinking and adaptation, promoting creative problem solving and conflict resolution. It allows children to build their own games, define their own rules, and develop the cognitive skills that are needed not only for athletics, but in every aspect of life.[15]

One of the **greatest differences between adults and children is that adults are goal oriented, and children are focused on immediate pleasure**. Adults see everything as leading toward something in the future - the big picture if you will - and thus tend to look at everything we do not simply for "how does this serve me now" but "how will this serve me in the future." As a result, we tend to look at play, with its focus on immediate gratification instead of long term goals, as a waste of time and an obstacle to long term growth. It might be getting in the way of things we want for our children in the future, so we tolerate it only to a point.

As a result, **we look down upon coaches who roll a ball out and say "go play."** We get angry when our soccer coach sits quietly on the bench, letting the kids work through their own problems, all bunched up in a giant blob, making mistakes without fear of repercussions and public correction, and playing a game that looks nothing like the adult version we see on TV.

We get upset that our coach does not teach kids positions, when in reality they do not possess the ability to understand a position until they understand positioning (do I need to provide depth, width, close support, etc.). In other words, **we have a long term goal in mind, and we want to get our kids to that goal as quickly and efficiently as possible.** Clearly by sitting there and not fixing the problem, our coach is delaying their development, right?

Wrong. The coach is doing it right. He is fostering development by helping them learn, and guiding their discovery of the answers rather than providing the answers. He gives them ideas in practice, but then lets them develop skill, creativity and critical thinking during the game. Everything that intuitively feels like inhibiting development is actually promoting it. We need to let them play!

More Thoughts on Diversification vs. Specialization in Youth Sports

Here are a few final thoughts on some of the advantages of a multi-sport background instead of early specialization:

1. **Better Overall Skills and Ability:** Research shows that early participation in multiple sports leads to better overall motor and athletic development, longer playing careers, increased ability to transfer sports skills other sports and increased motivation, ownership of the sports experience, and confidence.

2. **Smarter, More Creative Players**: Multi-sport participation at the youngest ages yields better decision making and pattern recognition, as well as increased creativity. There is evidence that athletes who are able to "read the game" in one sport are more apt to be equally adept in another, similar sport, and thus their ability transfers from one sport to another. These are all qualities that coaches of high level teams look for.

3. **Most College Athletes Come From a Multi-Sport Background**: A 2013 American Medical Society for Sports Medicine survey found that 88% of college athletes surveyed participated in more than one sport as a child.

4. **10,000 Hours is not a Rule**: In his survey of the scientific literature regarding sport specific practice in The Sports Gene, author David Epstein finds that most elite competitors require far less than 10,000 hours of deliberate practice. Specifically, studies have shown that basketball (4000 hours), field hockey (4000 hours) and wrestling (6000 hours) all require far less than 10,000 hours. Even Anders Ericsson, the researcher credited with discovering the 10,000 hour rule, says the misrepresentation of his work ignores many of the elements that go into high-performance (genetics, coaching, opportunity, luck) and focuses on only one, deliberate practice. That, he says, is wrong. (For more, here is an entire article I wrote on this)

5. **Free Play Equals More Play**: As mentioned above, early specialization ignores the importance of deliberate play. Researches found that activities which are intrinsically motivating, maximize fun and provide enjoyment are incredibly important. Deliberate play increases motor skills, emotional ability, and creativity. Children allowed deliberate play also tend spend more time engaged in a sport. Athletes in structured training with a coach spend a large amount of that time standing in line and waiting for coaches to set up activities and give instruction. In an hour of pickup basketball, children will usually spend the vast majority of the time playing, developing motor skills through the game, while research on training environments demonstrates that athletes' time on task varies between 25% to 54% of total training time. The **benefits of feedback from experienced coaches may be outweighed by the amount of time not spent** actually playing or practicing!

6. **There are Many Paths to Mastery**: Similar to the Steve Nash path and the Roger Federer path, studies in other sports seem to show that there are many paths to mastery. For instance, a 2003 study on professional ice hockey players found that while most pros had spent 10,000 hours or more involved in sports prior to age 20, only 3000 of those hours were involved in hockey specific deliberate practice (and only 450 of those hours were prior to age 12). The rest were spent in free play and other sports!

What Does This All Mean for Me?

You are now equipped with all the latest science and research regarding early sport specialization. You have access to my synopsis of many of the studies, as well as links to the actual research and articles if you choose to read them yourself. If it is time to make a decision for your child, you now can make a well informed one.

Perhaps you are asking "Where does John stand on this?"

While your decision is yours and yours alone, I feel it is only fair to let you know what I make of all the research I have read and experts I have had the chance to speak to regarding the current emphasis on early sport specialization. Here are my thoughts.

I believe that the evidence is quite compelling regarding the need for elite female gymnasts and figure skaters to specialize at a young age if they want to reach the upper echelons of their sport, for they reach their athletic peak in their teen years. But **for the vast majority of athletes, those who do not peak until their 20's, if you live in the United States, Canada, Australia or another country that has access to a wide variety of sports, your athletes are far better off sampling a variety of sports prior to age 14-16.**

The evidence tells me that an early diversification approach will have the following benefits for your athletes:

1. Reduce the risk of burnout and dropout.
2. Reduce the risk and rate of injuries.
3. Give your athlete a better chance to find enjoyment, autonomy and intrinsic motivation when it comes to sport.
4. Reduce the risk of your athlete developing maladaptive psychological behaviors, such as identifying their worth with their sport performance.
5. Allow your child to develop varied social networks, across a multitude of sports.
6. Allow your child to find their own passion, to identify a sport that fits their physical, psychological and social makeup, instead of what you think best fits them.
7. Improve the chances that your child becomes a lifelong athlete.
8. Give your child a balanced childhood -years he or she will never get back- before embarking upon the pursuit of higher athletic ambitions.

Various organizations throughout the United States advocate a similar, balanced approach. Organizations such as the Changing the Game Project, Bruce Brown's Proactive Coaching, the Positive Coaching Alliance and The Aspen Institute's Project Play have all been calling for a rethink of the current sports environment, and a more balanced approach to youth sports. I believe we need individual parents and coaches to advocate for this as well.

If your child is **under the age of 13, most experts believe it is crucial to participate in more than one sport**. When I get parents of 8 year olds who tell me "My son only likes soccer," I say "my son only likes macaroni and cheese, but I know that only eating macaroni and cheese is not necessarily good for him!" Maybe your son has never tried basketball, or he tried and had a bad coach or bad teammates. Do not be afraid to try again, because playing basketball can help him become a better soccer player through increased agility, balance, coordination and pattern awareness.

The more sports a child is introduced to, the better chance he has of **finding the one he is passionate about, taking ownership of it, and becoming a high-performer in it**. There is nothing wrong with a parent of a young athlete asking their child to try something, and if it does not work out, then so be it. The problem with early specialization is that many kids who have only played a single sport, at age 13 or so, say "I want to try something else."

If your child wants to play at the next level (and you want them to), **would it not be better to have a multi sport athlete decide to specialize in high school, instead of a specialist who decides to diversify in high school**? That is why athletes should diversify early. Explain to them how it helps them in their sport of choice. You will develop a better all around athlete, and potentially help a child appreciate his first sport, his coach and his team even more.

A young child certainly **does not need to participate in elite level competition in multiple sports.** Far too many well intentioned parents, in trying to ensure their child is not a single sport specialist, turn him into a multi-sport specialist, with swimming at 6am, soccer at 4pm and basketball at 7pm. I think **one organized sport per season**, especially for kids 10 and under (an age I selected, not researched based) is entirely appropriate.

By late middle school and high school, I think many athletes are mature enough, educated enough, and capable of having high aspirations and ambitions in a singular sport, and thus may choose to participate in only one organized sport. They may have jobs, significant others, musical or artistic pursuits, or a social life that only allows time for one high level sport. I think it is important that coaches, athletic directors, and parents ask these kids what their goals and ambitions are, instead of trying to determine them for them.

This does not mean theses athletes should not be encouraged to pursue other athletic interests. I coached many high level youth soccer players who only did one school/club sport, but loved to ski, bike, golf, and play ultimate Frisbee. This free play was a way to refresh and rejuvenate their body and mind after intense, high-level competition.

Athletes at this age also need a lot of rest, proper nutrition, academic balance, and general fitness. These days, many high school level sports are very competitive, a large time commitment, and are not for every athlete. We can respect their decision to only play one sport while helping them appropriately schedule their specialty sport training.

Some people may ask "Can't good coaching overcome many of the issues single sport specialization causes?" They point to the Lionel Messi's and Cristiano Ronaldo's of the soccer world as examples of people who only played soccer from a young age. This may be true, but they ignore three crucial points:

1. Many of Ronaldo and Messi's **early hours in the game consisted of free, deliberate play**. In free play, kids play multiple positions, and focus solely upon the enjoyment and fun of the sport. They are allowed to be creative, play fearlessly, and rely solely upon themselves for the motivation to pursue the sport. This is exactly the opposite of structured, organized training with a long term goal in mind, and has been scientifically shown to yield better overall athleticism.

2. Messi, Ronaldo and other high level soccer players were brought into the youth setup of very high level soccer organizations at a young age. These clubs, such as La Masia at FC Barcelona, have **dozens of full time staff attending to the needs of only 300 athletes. They have coaches, physicians, physiologists, nutritionists, chefs, psychologists, academic tutors, and more**. Every need is attended to, from proper training to medical attention to school to nutrition to rest. We have nothing similar in the United States, so to argue that we just need better educated coaches and then kids can specialize, because they do overseas, is comparing apples to oranges.

3. We cannot ignore the cultural differences that some athletes encounter, such as European or South American soccer players. The opportunity and encouragement to play multiple sports does not exist as it does in many places in the United States. In other countries, cultural forces push many of the best athletes toward a sport such as soccer, whereas in the US, top athletes have a multitude of choices. Again, it is not a like for like comparison.

To summarize my position, **a young athlete should experience many sports, and be given the chance to find one he or she is passionate about**. Limit their hours per week to their age. This will allow these athletes to reduce the risk of overuse injury, develop better athletically, and have a far likelier chance of continuing in sport throughout their life.

Kids can participate in multiple sports, but pursue one above the others as long as it is enjoyable, they own the experience, and they are the one motivated to play. Parents should encourage multi-sport participation for the good of the athlete, while understanding that early introduction and developing sport specific skills is important in many sports prior to your child's growth spurt. We know the science, so it is our role at times to do things that our kids may not want to do because they do not have the knowledge, maturity and perspective to make that decision. In other words, if they did not like reading, wouldn't you still make them learn to read because it is a necessary life skill? We can think of multi-sport participation the same way.

By high school, if an athlete wants to pursue a single sport, we should support that decision, but ensure that the athlete lives a balanced life, gets the proper rest, nutrition, and time away from sport.

And last but not least, we should never forget that the majority of professional athletes were multi-sport participants as kids!

How Do I Deal With Coaches Who Force My Child to Decide?

Ah yes, the million dollar question. What do you do when you have studied the science, discussed everything with your athlete, and then you come across a coach or an organization that could care less?

This is the most difficult situation you may face, and there is no one size fits all answer. Depending upon the level of play of your child, the number of sporting options in your town, the difference in coaching between different levels, and a whole host of factors, everyone's situation is different. It is not easy to choose between deciding to forgo play at a travel club for an elite young athlete, and instead playing at a recreational level that a child finds unchallenging and not the least bit motivating. It is not easy to choose between the highly qualified coach who provides a strong training environment, and a parent coached team that simply does not supply the same experience.

In the long term, our mission at the Changing the game Project is to help sports organizations realize that it should not be an either or situation. Great coaches should be developing better all around athletes by encouraging multi-sport participation at young ages, and creating player-centered organizations that follow the best science, psychology, and LTAD principles. I ask you to pass this book onto them, because there are many, many fantastic coaches who have never been shown any of this science or psychology.

But today it's your child who has to decide. You don't have ten years; you may only have 10 days to decide. These are the letters I get all the time, the ones which prompted me to write this book. Here is what I suggest.

Have a conversation with your coach or organization. Share this information with them, and ask them if they were given a choice between the following two scenarios, what would they choose?

Scenario 1: A sports environment that is scientifically based, and shown in academic study to produce healthy athletes who move with confidence, are more skilled and competent competitors, become children who are more likely to be successful on and off the field, and are more likely to gain enjoyment from sport.

Or…

Scenario 2: A sports environment that academic study has shown is more likely to produce less athletically talented kids, reduced skill development, less success on and off the field, and a much higher rate of burnout and other psychological issues.

As you have probably figured out, Scenario 1 is a multi-sport, player-centered developmental environment that is based upon LTAD best practices, and lowers the chances of an athlete having the physical, social and psychological issues that often cause burnout and dropout. It is the scenario we advocate at the Changing the Game Project, one that gets the most kids involved in sport, and produces the most high level athletes.

Scenario 2 is the real world for far too many people. It is the requirement to commit early to a single sport, put in many hours of deliberate practice in the pre-teen years, as well as extensive travel and often an environment focused upon results. It is a scenario that leads to many physical, social and psychological issues. It is a scenario created by the "youth sports as a for profit business" environment we live in. And it is less likely to help your child than scenario 1. Yet it is sometimes the only choice…

Unless we take a stand and start to find another way…

Unless we tell a coach that we will commit to this but need time away…

Unless we tell a coach that science tells us every child needs a break…

Unless we forget that we are not just developing athletes; we are developing people who needs these sport skills to also become life skills.

Until enough of us take a stand for what is right, we will continue to take our kids down a path that is wrong for far too many. I have not had to ever make this choice, but someday I likely will. When I do, I will follow my child's lead, but I will also follow the science, and follow my heart.

What if My Child Has Already Specialized?

According to Michael Sagas of the University of Florida, if your only goal for your child or team is to have immediate age-group success and win early and often, then an early sport specialization path is the right one. Such a path may lead to early selection to all-star teams, increased short-term self esteem, and a better chance of a higher level of competition early on. Sadly, many families feel forced down this path, for these very reasons. If they do not specialize early, they fear that their child's chance at playing a sport at an elite level may be gone. This fear is not entirely unjustified, and that is exactly what is wrong with American youth sports. It is exactly why we all need to take a stand.

We need to stand up for our children because Sagas, like many others, has found that "**beyond the few benefits or specific contexts outlined above, the majority of the literature suggests that early specialization can have significant negative consequences on the development of an athlete over time**." As we have discussed, these may range from higher injury and dropout rates to social isolation, shorter playing careers, less enjoyment, limited motor development, and perhaps worst of all, decreased athletic participation as an adult.[16]

If your child has already gone down the path of early specialization, and perhaps is even a top performer, you face your own challenges. It is wise to remember that statistics show only about 10% of elite 10 year old athletes players are still elite at 18, and only 8% of Nobel Prize winners and world champions were child prodigies. In fact, the only thing that early success guarantees is…early success.

If your child is an early high-achiever, here are five tips:

1. **Recognize their current achievement, but put it in context**:
   Young players whom are better than their teammates often know that they are. Some are comfortable with the attention; others struggle in the limelight. Our job as adults is to recognize this and help the athletes deal with this situation. Parents should discuss with them the social implications and see if they are affecting your child. Note the reasons why they are doing well, be aware of jealousy from other players, and DO NOT add drama to the team. Take your own ego out of it, and let the game belong to your child. "We" did not score 3 goals, he did. "We" did not win the tournament, she did.

2. **Praise Them for Effort and Focus:**
   Make sure they adhere to your standards. One of the biggest issues I see is when coaches and parents praise little Johnny for being great, for being the best. Do not praise ability! Praise things he can control, such as his effort and focus. Talent gets you nowhere without effort, yet often young elite players are not required to put in maximum effort or focus in training and games in order to be successful. Parents can encourage a growth mindset in their kids by focusing on their effort, not their ability. They are far more likely to be successful in the long term if their attitude is "I am good because I work hard" than "I am good." Do not ignore poor effort just because they won, and be sure to acknowledge a great effort in a loss.

3. **Encourage them to make others better:**
   Being an elite young player is an opportunity to be a leader. Players naturally look up to the top performers, and it is never too young to start teaching basic leadership. Parents can remind their kids that being a leader comes with responsibility. Team captain is not just about flipping a coin and picking which side you will defend first. It is about making your teammates better, positively inspiring them and helping them to overcome mistakes. It is about humility, and making sure their teammates are recognized for things that might not make the score sheet.

4. **Find them opportunities to be challenged**
   Perhaps one of the biggest detriments of our current set up is that the focus upon results holds back elite performers "for the good of the team." Players who would benefit by playing up an age group, or at least getting some games with an older team, are often held back to help their own age group. Parents, please talk to your coach and/or club director, and find kids camps, training sessions, or just pick up games with older players that will push them. If they are physically more gifted than their own age group, find a place for them to compete with players

who share similar physical traits, where they learn quickly that technique matters! So many players are allowed to rely solely upon physical gifts, and once this advantage dissipates, they have never developed the technique to advance. Teach them that their physical advantages are only temporary.

5. **Love them for who they are, not what they do**

Perhaps the most damaging thing that can happen to a talented young athlete is that his or her entire identity and self worth becomes tied to sports performance. When things are going well, all is great, but when they start to struggle – all elite athletes do – do you still love them? Do you treat them the same? Do they realize that sports are something that they do, not who they are?

Parents, you must encourage your kids to have a life outside of sports, whether it is music, art, theater, family and friends, you name it, just do not allow their entire life to become about sports. If they are good enough, eventually that may happen, but it should not when they are very young. Make sure they get time off, do not cancel every family reunion or vacation for soccer tournaments, and make sure they participate in other activities to reduce burn out and overuse injuries. And finally, each and every time they play, remind them how much you love watching them play, and then go get lunch or a smoothie!

Final Thoughts

If you have not yet gone down the single sport path, and if you are making the decision about when and where to specialize, I hope I have provided you with the knowledge and confidence to make the best decisions for your child and your family. Remember that all the great benefits that you see for your child if he or she performs at an elite level might not be apparent to your child; even if they are, your athlete might not value them like you do.

Remember that before you make any decisions, you must communicate with your athlete. Sit down with her, and discuss goals, aspirations, and realistic expectations (click here for NCAA statistics on the likelihood of getting a scholarship). Also remember how incredible high school sports can be, and the ability to perform in multiple sports in front of your best friends is a once in a lifetime opportunity. This may matter to your child far more than any thought of scholarships or collegiate play.

Please remember in making your decisions that your child's high-level sports career will likely only last 25% of his or her life. On the other hand, **the lessons they learn, and their relationship with you, their parent, must last a lifetime.** Your knowledge and wisdom as an adult can guide your child down a path that not only gives them a great chance at becoming an elite performer, but more importantly, an elite human being.

Finally, please take to heart these words from Sweden's Minister for Culture and Sport Lena Adelsohn Liljeroth in the opening remarks of the May 2014 Research Conference on Children and Youth in Sport:

"There is no medal worth more than a lost childhood."

It is up to us as parents and coaches of young athletes to ensure that our children never have to choose between being a child and being an athlete.

Our athletes need responsible parents and coaches more than ever before. If you have come this far, you have already done them a great service.

Good luck with your journey. Perhaps I will see you on the field.

Recommended Additional Reading

Istvan Bayli. Long Term Athlete Development. Human Kinetics, 2013. The bible of the LTAD movement.

Joseph Baker, Stephen Cobley and Jessica Fraser-Thomas, "What do we know about early sport specialization? Not much!." *High Ability Studies*, Volume 20, No. 1, June 2009, 77-89. This is a great review of existing literature on the subject, along with another article by Baker, "Early specialization in youth sport: A requirement for adult expertise?" 2003: High Ability Studies, 14, 85-94.

Dan Coyle. The Talent Code: Greatness Isn't Born. It's Grown. Here's How. Bantam Books, 2009.

Brooke De Lench, "Early Sports Specialization: Does it Lead to Long Term Problems?" found at www.momsteam.com

David Epstein. The Sports Gene: Inside The Science of Extraordinary Athletic Performance. New York: The Penguin Group, 2014

Bobby Orr. Bobby Orr: My Story. GP Putnam and Sons, 2013. This is perhaps the best sports biography I have read about an athlete who was elite, played for pure enjoyment, participated in multiple sports while pursuing one passionately, owned the experience, and had extraordinary parents who let the sport belong to him. Read this!

Michael Sagas, "What Does the Science Say About Athletic Development in Children?" University of Florida Sport Policy and Research Collaborative research Brief for the Aspen Institute Sports and Society Program.

Ross Tucker, whose blog at www.TheSportScientists.com is a must read for anyone interested in Sport Science. Try these two articles "Early vs Late Specialization: When should children specialize in sport?" and "Specialization, Training Volume and Talent Development."

Matthew Shomper. "Benefits of Multiple-Sport Participation Outweigh Sport Specialization." High School Today, May 2011. You can access the article here: http://www.iahsaa.org/wp-content/uploads/2013/08/Multiple_Sport_Participation_Benefits.pdf

(Author's Note: All book links throughout the booklet are Amazon Affiliate links where applicable, and the author receives a small percentage of the sale.)

Notes:

[1] David Epstein. The Sports Gene: Inside The Science of Extraordinary Athletic Performance. New York: The Penguin Group, 2014, 297-298. The story of Nash and Federer appear only in the paperback edition of the book.

[2] http://www.aspenprojectplay.org/about-project-play

[3] Joseph Baker, Stephen Cobley and Jessica Fraser-Thomas, "What do we know about early sport specialization? Not much!." High Ability Studies, Volume 20, No. 1, June 2009, 77-89.

[4] The full LTAD program can be found on the website of The Canadian Sport For Life Foundation, www.canadiansportforlife.ca, if you would like more information or in Istvan Balyi's book Long Term Athlete Development.

[5] The vast majority of the section on LTAD has been excerpted from John O'Sullivan. Changing the Game: The Parent's Guide to Raising Happy, High-Performing Athletes and Giving Youth Sports Back to Our Kids. New York: Morgan James, 2014.

[6] Brooke De Lench, "Early Sports Specialization: Does it Lead to Long Term Problems?" www.momsteam.com

[7] See Danny Knobler. 'Baseball's Pitching Dilemma: Too Hard, Too Fast, Too Much, Too Soon." http://bleacherreport.com/articles/2080837-baseballs-pitching-dilemma-too-hard-too-fast-too-much-too-soon?

[8] The best resource for Concussion and Youth Sports Injuries is Moms Team. You can get lost here for days reading all the links and research. http://www.momsteam.com/health-safety/concussion-safety.

[9] Referenced from http://www.aspenprojectplay.org//the-facts

[10] Baker, Cobley and Fraser-Thomas, p. 80.

[11] Baker, Cobley and Fraser-Thomas, p. 81.

[12] Kevin Hellicker, "The Problem for Sports parents: Overspending." Wall Street Journal May 12, 2014 http://online.wsj.com/news/articles/SB10001424052702303851804579558103723377142

[13] Coakley, J. (1992). Burnout among adolescent athletes: A personal failure or social problem? Sociology of Sport Journal, 9, 271-285.

[14] Michael Sagas, "What Does the Science Say About Athletic Development in Children?" University of Florida Sport Policy and Research Collaborative research Brief for the Aspen Institute Sports and Society Program.

[15] http://www.thesportinmind.com/articles/practice-or-play-in-sport-what-is-best-for-creating-champions/

[16] Sagas, 2.

41533804R00018

Made in the USA
Middletown, DE
16 March 2017